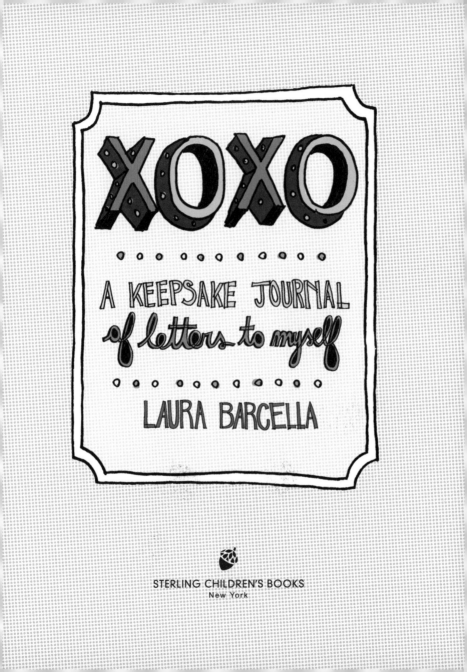

XOXO

A KEEPSAKE JOURNAL
of letters to myself

LAURA BARCELLA

STERLING CHILDREN'S BOOKS
New York

STERLING CHILDREN'S BOOKS
New York

An Imprint of Sterling Publishing
1166 Avenue of the Americas
New York, NY 10036

ISBN 978-1-4549-1824-0

Distributed in Canada by Sterling Publishing
c/o Canadian Manda Group, 664 Annette Street
Toronto, Ontario, Canada M6S 2C8.
Distributed in the United Kingdom by GMC Distribution Services
Castle Place, 166 High Street, Lewes, East Sussex, England BN7 1XU
Distributed in Australia by Capricorn Link (Australia) Pty. Ltd.
P.O. Box 704, Windsor, NSW 2756, Australia

For information about custom editions, special sales, and premium and corporate purchases,
please contact Sterling Special Sales at 800-805-5489 or specialsales@sterlingpublishing.com.

Cover illustration by Bethany Robertson
Design by 3&Co.

Manufactured in China

Lot #:
2 4 6 8 10 9 7 5 3 1
01/16

www.sterlingpublishing.com

Well, hey there!

This book you're holding in your hands is a special kind of journal made just for you. But guess what? It's much, MUCH more than just a plain lined notebook or a musty old diary. *XOXO* is a special place for you to write letters to yourself. Yes, letters FOR you, BY you. That might sound a little strange, but we promise, it's actually really fun and rewarding!

This is a place where you can be utterly real about all the awesome (and not so awesome) elements of your crazy life. By writing letters to your future self about who you are today, *XOXO* will help you reflect on your life. It will encourage you to jot down all kinds of fun thoughts about the greatest subject on Earth: why yes, that'd be you. And when you've finished, you can tuck this book away so that when you pick it up in ten or twenty years, you'll have a super-detailed glimpse at all the stuff you thought, felt, did, and believed when you were younger.

Look at this book as a sort of trail of breadcrumbs for your future self. A personal, heartfelt, totally unique glimpse into everything special about the YOU you are today (and all the yous that came before)!

Now, find a quiet corner to hang in, grab a cup of hot cocoa or something else suitably delicious, and start writing some letters to the one person you'll always know best:

YOU!

**Write a letter to yourself about the
best day you've ever had.**

St Vincent De Paul
905 - ~~ 88~~ 932 - 1145.
Make appt for Monday to
go on tuesday for food
Volucher. $40.⁰⁰ Grant tiger or
food Basics.

Community Care. for
food & Clothing
905 - 685 - 1340

Write a letter to yourself about your favorite pet—either your own or someone else's.

N R H	$20.00
Meal w	140.00
Meal w G. Tiger	150.00
Dan	100.00
Flower seeds	40.00
Coffee	100.00
G. Tiger	150.00
Tax	50.00
	70.00
	1025.00

1,500
1,025
2 4/7 5,

Write a letter to yourself about the best dream you ever had.

_____

_____

_____

_____

_____

_____

_____

_____

_____

_____

_____

_____

_____

_____

_____

_____

_____

Write a letter to yourself about the
worst dream you ever had.

Write a letter to yourself about the funniest story anyone's ever told you.

_____

_____

_____

_____

_____

_____

_____

_____

_____

_____

_____

_____

_____

_____

_____

_____

Write a letter to yourself about the fateful day you met your first crush.

_____

_____

_____

_____

_____

_____

_____

_____

_____

_____

_____

_____

_____

_____

_____

_____

_____

_____

_____

Write a letter to yourself about your first kiss. If you haven't had one yet, what do you hope it will be like?

Write a letter to yourself about the outfit you'd wear to the party of the century!

_____

_____

_____

_____

_____

_____

_____

_____

_____

_____

_____

_____

_____

_____

Write a letter to yourself about what you'd want your first home to look like.

_____

_____

_____

_____

_____

_____

_____

_____

_____

_____

_____

_____

_____

_____

_____

_____

_____

_____

_____

Write a letter to yourself about what you might want your college major to be, and why.

**Write a letter to yourself about what you'd do
if you won a $5 million lottery.**

Write a letter to yourself about what you
want your first car to be.

_____

_____

_____

_____

_____

_____

_____

_____

_____

_____

_____

_____

_____

_____

_____

_____

_____

_____

_____

Write a letter to yourself about your dream vacation.

_____

_____

_____

_____

_____

_____

_____

_____

_____

_____

_____

_____

_____

_____

_____

_____

_____

Write a letter to yourself about the most embarrassing thing that's ever happened to you at school.

_____

_____

_____

_____

_____

_____

_____

_____

_____

_____

_____

_____

_____

_____

Write a letter to yourself about the most embarrassing
thing that's ever happened to you in front of your family.

_____

_____

_____

_____

_____

_____

_____

_____

_____

_____

_____

_____

_____

_____

_____

_____

Write a letter to yourself about the most exciting day you've ever had with your family.

Write a letter to yourself about the worst fight you ever had with your parents.

_____

_____

_____

_____

_____

_____

_____

_____

_____

_____

_____

_____

_____

_____

_____

_____

_____

Write a letter to yourself about the worst fight you ever had with your best friend.

Write a letter to yourself about the top five
qualities you look for in a friend.

_____

_____

_____

_____

_____

_____

_____

_____

_____

_____

_____

_____

_____

_____

_____

_____

Write a letter to yourself about the best possible thing you can imagine happening to you this year.

_____

_____

_____

_____

_____

_____

_____

_____

_____

_____

_____

_____

_____

_____

Write a letter to yourself about what makes
you special on the inside.

Write a letter to yourself about what makes you special on the outside.

_____

_____

_____

_____

_____

_____

_____

_____

_____

_____

_____

_____

_____

_____

_____

Write a letter to yourself about astronauts.
Would you want to go up in space one day?

Write a letter to yourself about something you're good at . . . that no one else knows about.

Write a letter to yourself about your favorite actor.

Write a letter to yourself about your worst
experience at a doctor's office.

_____

_____

_____

_____

_____

_____

_____

_____

_____

_____

_____

_____

_____

_____

_____

_____

_____

_____

_____

Write a letter to yourself about your very first celeb crush.

Write a letter to yourself about a sport you're good at . . . and one you're not so good at.

_____

_____

_____

_____

_____

_____

_____

_____

_____

_____

_____

_____

_____

_____

_____

_____

_____

_____

_____

Write a letter to yourself about the best compliment you've ever gotten.

_____

_____

_____

_____

_____

_____

_____

_____

_____

_____

_____

_____

_____

_____

_____

_____

_____

_____

Write a letter to yourself about your fave relative.

Write a letter to yourself about your favorite city.

Write a letter to yourself about ghosts.
Do you believe in them?

**Write a letter to yourself about how
you feel about social media.**

_____

_____

_____

_____

_____

_____

_____

_____

_____

_____

_____

_____

_____

_____

_____

_____

_____

_____

_____

_____

_____

**Write a letter to yourself about your favorite—
or least favorite—memory of being at the beach.**

_____

_____

_____

_____

_____

_____

_____

_____

_____

_____

_____

_____

_____

_____

_____

_____

_____

Write a letter to yourself about your favorite
thing to do on snow days.

_____

_____

_____

_____

_____

_____

_____

_____

_____

_____

_____

_____

_____

_____

_____

Write a letter to yourself
about rainy days.

_____

_____

_____

_____

_____

_____

_____

_____

_____

_____

_____

_____

_____

_____

_____

_____

_____

_____

Write a letter to yourself about the most embarrassing accessory (necklace, tie, belt, whatever!) your mom's ever put on you.

_____
_____
_____
_____
_____
_____
_____
_____
_____
_____
_____
_____
_____
_____
_____
_____
_____
_____
_____

Write a letter to yourself about the last
meal you'd wanna eat before you die.

_____

_____

_____

_____

_____

_____

_____

_____

_____

_____

_____

_____

_____

_____

_____

_____

Write a letter to yourself about where you'd go on a weekend road trip with your BFF.

_____

_____

_____

_____

_____

_____

_____

_____

_____

_____

_____

_____

_____

_____

_____

_____

_____

_____

Write a letter to yourself about whether you're more of an introvert or an extrovert.

Write a letter to yourself outlining your best idea for a novel you'd write.

_____

_____

_____

_____

_____

_____

_____

_____

_____

_____

_____

_____

_____

_____

_____

_____

_____

Write a letter to yourself about your number-one can't-miss TV show.

_____

_____

_____

_____

_____

_____

_____

_____

_____

_____

_____

_____

_____

_____

_____

_____

_____

_____

_____

_____

Write a letter to yourself about your feelings about karaoke. What's your go-to karaoke song?

_____
_____
_____
_____
_____
_____
_____
_____
_____
_____
_____
_____
_____
_____
_____
_____
_____
_____

What kind of wedding would you want to have one day? Write a letter to yourself describing it!

**Write a letter to yourself about your thoughts on death.
What do you think might happen after we die?**

_____

_____

_____

_____

_____

_____

_____

_____

_____

_____

_____

_____

_____

_____

_____

_____

_____

_____

Write a letter to yourself about the worst insult you've ever gotten.

_____

_____

_____

_____

_____

_____

_____

_____

_____

_____

_____

_____

_____

_____

_____

_____

_____

_____

Write a letter to yourself about a time you drifted away from a friend.

Write a letter to yourself about your favorite word.

_____

_____

_____

_____

_____

_____

_____

_____

_____

_____

_____

_____

_____

_____

_____

_____

_____

_____

_____

Write a letter to yourself about your fave song or album to listen to when you're feeling down.

Write a letter to yourself about the weirdest adventure you've ever had all by yourself.

_____

_____

_____

_____

_____

_____

_____

_____

_____

_____

_____

_____

_____

_____

_____

_____

_____

Write a letter to yourself about the meanest thing
you've ever said to someone.

_____

_____

_____

_____

_____

_____

_____

_____

_____

_____

_____

_____

_____

_____

_____

_____

Write a letter to yourself about the worst day you can remember.

**Write a letter to yourself about the job you'd do
if you couldn't do your dream job.**

_____

_____

_____

_____

_____

_____

_____

_____

_____

_____

_____

_____

_____

_____

_____

_____

_____

Write a letter to yourself about fame.
Would you want to be famous?

_____

_____

_____

_____

_____

_____

_____

_____

_____

_____

_____

_____

_____

_____

_____

_____

_____

_____

Write a letter to yourself about your fave holiday.

Write a letter to yourself about your perfect beauty product.

Write a letter to yourself about the best clothing trend of last year.

_____

_____

_____

_____

_____

_____

_____

_____

_____

_____

_____

_____

_____

_____

_____

_____

_____

_____

Write a letter to yourself about the worst clothing trend of last year.

_____

_____

_____

_____

_____

_____

_____

_____

_____

_____

_____

_____

_____

_____

_____

_____

_____

_____

_____

Write a letter to yourself about the chore you'd most like to never ever do again.

Write a letter to yourself about the
strangest thing you ever saw go down
inside your house.

_____

_____

_____

_____

_____

_____

_____

_____

_____

_____

_____

_____

_____

_____

_____

_____

_____

_____

Write a letter to yourself about your most irritating relative.

_____

_____

_____

_____

_____

_____

_____

_____

_____

_____

_____

_____

_____

_____

_____

_____

_____

Write a letter to yourself about the animal that scares you most.

_____

_____

_____

_____

_____

_____

_____

_____

_____

_____

_____

_____

_____

_____

_____

_____

_____

Write a letter to yourself about the cutest boy or girl you've ever seen in person.

_____

_____

_____

_____

_____

_____

_____

_____

_____

_____

_____

_____

_____

_____

_____

_____

_____

Write a letter to yourself about the person whose style you most want to steal.

Write a letter to yourself about the worst time you got sick.

_____

_____

_____

_____

_____

_____

_____

_____

_____

_____

_____

_____

_____

_____

_____

_____

Write a letter to yourself about a time you did something totally out of character.

_____

_____

_____

_____

_____

_____

_____

_____

_____

_____

_____

_____

_____

_____

_____

_____

_____

_____

_____

Write a letter to yourself about your favorite character from a book or story.

Write a letter to yourself about how you feel
about the great outdoors.

_____

_____

_____

_____

_____

_____

_____

_____

_____

_____

_____

_____

_____

_____

Write a letter to yourself about summer camp.

Write a letter to yourself about jealousy.
Who are you jealous of?

_____

_____

_____

_____

_____

_____

_____

_____

_____

_____

_____

_____

_____

_____

_____

_____

_____

_____

Write a letter to yourself about your favorite movie and why it's so great.

Write a letter to yourself about swimming.
How do you feel about it?

_____
_____
_____
_____
_____
_____
_____
_____
_____
_____
_____
_____
_____
_____
_____
_____
_____
_____

Write a letter to yourself about your fave summer-vacation memory.

_____

_____

_____

_____

_____

_____

_____

_____

_____

_____

_____

_____

_____

_____

_____

_____

_____

_____

_____

Write a letter to yourself about the kind
of bug that freaks you out most.

_____

_____

_____

_____

_____

_____

_____

_____

_____

_____

_____

_____

_____

_____

_____

_____

Write a letter to yourself about how you feel about your looks.

_____

_____

_____

_____

_____

_____

_____

_____

_____

_____

_____

_____

_____

_____

_____

_____

_____

_____

Write a letter to yourself about something other people are afraid of that you're not.

Write a letter to yourself about your fave kind of candy.

_____

_____

_____

_____

_____

_____

_____

_____

_____

_____

_____

_____

_____

_____

_____

_____

_____

_____

Write a letter to yourself about the best birthday you've ever had.

_____
_____
_____
_____
_____
_____
_____
_____
_____
_____
_____
_____
_____
_____
_____
_____
_____

Write a letter to yourself about a time you
felt betrayed by someone close to you.

Write a letter to yourself about the first time
one of your crushes ever spoke to you.

_____

_____

_____

_____

_____

_____

_____

_____

_____

_____

_____

_____

_____

_____

_____

Write a letter to yourself about the happiest
memory you have from school.

Write a letter to yourself about your earliest memory ever.

_____

_____

_____

_____

_____

_____

_____

_____

_____

_____

_____

_____

_____

_____

_____

_____

_____

Write a letter to yourself about the greatest teacher you ever had.

Write a letter to yourself about a
person who inspires you.

_____

_____

_____

_____

_____

_____

_____

_____

_____

_____

_____

_____

_____

_____

_____

_____

_____

_____

_____

Write a letter to yourself about your musical skills or the musical skills you wish you had!

_____

_____

_____

_____

_____

_____

_____

_____

_____

_____

_____

_____

_____

_____

_____

_____

Write a letter to yourself about the top five
things you'd bring to a desert island.

_____

_____

_____

_____

_____

_____

_____

_____

_____

_____

_____

_____

_____

_____

_____

_____

Write a letter to yourself about a song that reminds you of an amazing time in your life.

Write a letter to yourself about a song that reminds you of something sad.

Write a letter to yourself about what kind of magazine you'd create if you decided to make your own magazine.

_____

_____

_____

_____

_____

_____

_____

_____

_____

_____

_____

_____

_____

_____

_____

_____

_____

_____

Write a letter to yourself about the kind of music you'd make if you decided to start your own band. What would you sound like?

_____

_____

_____

_____

_____

_____

_____

_____

_____

_____

_____

_____

_____

_____

_____

_____

_____

_____

_____

_____

Write a letter to yourself about your favorite genre of film.

Write a letter to yourself about who you'd want to portray you in a movie of your life, and why you picked them!

Write a letter to yourself about your favorite after-school activity.

_____

_____

_____

_____

_____

_____

_____

_____

_____

_____

_____

_____

_____

_____

_____

_____

_____

_____

Write a letter to yourself about the grossest time you ever puked.

_____

_____

_____

_____

_____

_____

_____

_____

_____

_____

_____

_____

_____

_____

_____

_____

_____

_____

Write a letter to yourself about the era you would most like to visit if you could go back in time.

Write a letter to yourself about the best thing **EVER CREATED** (peanut butter? hair dryers? cell phones?).

_____

_____

_____

_____

_____

_____

_____

_____

_____

_____

_____

_____

_____

_____

_____

_____

_____

_____

Write a letter to yourself about a fantastic invention YOU'D create.

_____

_____

_____

_____

_____

_____

_____

_____

_____

_____

_____

_____

_____

_____

_____

_____

_____

_____

_____

Write a letter to yourself about the three people you'd most like to invite to dinner (dead or alive, famous or nonfamous!).

_____

_____

_____

_____

_____

_____

_____

_____

_____

_____

_____

_____

_____

_____

_____

_____

_____

_____

Write a letter to yourself about an activity you totally lose yourself in.

_____

_____

_____

_____

_____

_____

_____

_____

_____

_____

_____

_____

_____

_____

_____

_____

_____

_____

Write a letter to yourself about your most beloved
hand-me-down from a parent or sibling.

Write a letter to yourself about your most fantastic hair accessory.

_____

_____

_____

_____

_____

_____

_____

_____

_____

_____

_____

_____

_____

_____

_____

_____

_____

Write a letter to yourself about what birthday gift you'd totally ask for if money weren't an object.

_____

_____

_____

_____

_____

_____

_____

_____

_____

_____

_____

_____

_____

_____

_____

_____

_____

_____

_____

_____

Write a letter to yourself about your favorite color combination.

Write a letter to yourself about what you love
most about your crush's face.

_____

_____

_____

_____

_____

_____

_____

_____

_____

_____

_____

_____

_____

_____

_____

_____

Write a letter to yourself about the number-one
best thing about your BFF.

Write a letter to yourself about the number-one best thing about your mom or dad.

_____

_____

_____

_____

_____

_____

_____

_____

_____

_____

_____

_____

_____

_____

_____

_____

_____

_____

Write a letter to yourself about your worst enemy
and why they suck so much.

_____

_____

_____

_____

_____

_____

_____

_____

_____

_____

_____

_____

_____

_____

_____

_____

Write a letter to yourself about
the habit that annoys you most
when other people do it.

_____

_____

_____

_____

_____

_____

_____

_____

_____

_____

_____

_____

_____

_____

_____

_____

_____

_____

Write a letter to yourself about your mom or dad's most annoying habit.

Write a letter to yourself about the last thing that made you LOL.

_____

_____

_____

_____

_____

_____

_____

_____

_____

_____

_____

_____

_____

_____

_____

_____

_____

_____

Write a letter to yourself about the last
movie that made you cry.

_____

_____

_____

_____

_____

_____

_____

_____

_____

_____

_____

_____

_____

_____

_____

_____

_____

_____

_____

_____

_____

Write a letter to yourself about the thing that makes you feel saddest when you think about it.

_____

_____

_____

_____

_____

_____

_____

_____

_____

_____

_____

_____

_____

_____

_____

_____

_____

_____

_____

Write a letter to yourself about how you feel about eating meat.

_____

_____

_____

_____

_____

_____

_____

_____

_____

_____

_____

_____

_____

_____

_____

_____

_____

_____

Write a letter to yourself about what you like most about being a kid.

_____

_____

_____

_____

_____

_____

_____

_____

_____

_____

_____

_____

_____

_____

_____

_____

_____

_____

_____

_____

Write a letter to yourself about the worst advice you've ever gotten.

Write a letter to yourself about the best
advice you've ever gotten.

Write a letter to yourself about what you'd most like to tell your crush . . . but can't.

_____

_____

_____

_____

_____

_____

_____

_____

_____

_____

_____

_____

_____

_____

_____

_____

_____

_____

Write a letter to yourself about city versus small-town living. Which do you prefer?

_____

_____

_____

_____

_____

_____

_____

_____

_____

_____

_____

_____

_____

_____

_____

_____

_____

_____

_____

Write a letter to yourself about how you feel about hugs.

Write a letter to yourself about the coolest
part of your day today.

_____

_____

_____

_____

_____

_____

_____

_____

_____

_____

_____

_____

_____

_____

_____

_____

_____

_____

_____

Write a letter to yourself about your fave month and why you dig it.

_____

_____

_____

_____

_____

_____

_____

_____

_____

_____

_____

_____

_____

_____

_____

_____

**Write a letter to yourself about a trip
you really want to take.**

_____

_____

_____

_____

_____

_____

_____

_____

_____

_____

_____

_____

_____

_____

_____

_____

Write a letter to yourself about a time you laughed when you probably shouldn't have.

_____

_____

_____

_____

_____

_____

_____

_____

_____

_____

_____

_____

_____

_____

_____

_____

Write a letter to yourself about what you're most excited about right this second.

_____

_____

_____

_____

_____

_____

_____

_____

_____

_____

_____

_____

_____

_____

_____

_____

_____

_____

Write a letter to yourself about bubble baths versus showers.

Write a letter to yourself about a time you felt like you didn't fit in.

_____

_____

_____

_____

_____

_____

_____

_____

_____

_____

_____

_____

_____

_____

_____

_____

_____

Write a letter to yourself about a skill you wish you were better at.

Write a letter to yourself about your fave comedian
(or the funniest person you know).

_____

_____

_____

_____

_____

_____

_____

_____

_____

_____

_____

_____

_____

Write a letter to yourself about what you'd change if your parents let you redo your bedroom however you wanted.

_____

_____

_____

_____

_____

_____

_____

_____

_____

_____

_____

_____

_____

_____

_____

_____

_____

Write a letter to yourself about how you feel about having kids. Would you like to have them one day? What are some rules you'd give them?

_____

_____

_____

_____

_____

_____

_____

_____

_____

_____

_____

_____

_____

_____

_____

_____

_____

_____

Write a letter to yourself about your biggest pet peeve.

Write a letter to yourself about any ways you've noticed that girls and boys are treated differently. Does it bug you?

_____

_____

_____

_____

_____

_____

_____

_____

_____

_____

_____

_____

_____

_____

_____

_____

_____

Write a letter to yourself about your least favorite place on Earth.

Write a letter to yourself about something that annoys you about being your age.

_____

_____

_____

_____

_____

_____

_____

_____

_____

_____

_____

_____

_____

_____

_____

_____

Write a letter to yourself about what animal you'd
be if you could be any kind of animal.

_____

_____

_____

_____

_____

_____

_____

_____

_____

_____

_____

_____

_____

_____

_____

_____

_____

Write a letter to yourself about what your dream house looks like.

_____

_____

_____

_____

_____

_____

_____

_____

_____

_____

_____

_____

_____

_____

_____

_____

_____

_____

_____

Write a letter to yourself about a time you wished you could just disappear.

Write a letter to yourself about the grossest thing you ever saw a friend do.

_____

_____

_____

_____

_____

_____

_____

_____

_____

_____

_____

_____

_____

Write a letter to yourself about your earliest memory of a family friend.

_____

_____

_____

_____

_____

_____

_____

_____

_____

_____

_____

_____

_____

_____

_____

_____

Write a letter to yourself about what song you'd
choose as the theme song for your life.

Write a letter to yourself about the character from
a movie, book, cartoon, or anything else that you'd
most like to be BFFs with in real life.

Write a letter to yourself about the food that most makes you wanna puke.

_____
_____
_____
_____
_____
_____
_____
_____
_____
_____
_____
_____
_____
_____
_____
_____
_____
_____

Write a letter to yourself about what your dream day spent in nature would look like.

_____
_____
_____
_____
_____
_____
_____
_____
_____
_____
_____
_____
_____
_____
_____
_____

Write a letter to yourself about what God or religion means to you (if they mean anything at all!).

_____

_____

_____

_____

_____

_____

_____

_____

_____

_____

_____

_____

_____

_____

_____

_____

Write a letter to yourself about what you think about heaven and hell. Do they exist?

_____

_____

_____

_____

_____

_____

_____

_____

_____

_____

_____

_____

_____

_____

_____

_____

_____

Write a letter to yourself about the best
night's sleep you ever had.

_____

_____

_____

_____

_____

_____

_____

_____

_____

_____

_____

_____

_____

_____

_____

_____

Write a letter to yourself about sleep in general. How much do you love it? Do you sleep late or wake up early?

_____
_____
_____
_____
_____
_____
_____
_____
_____
_____
_____
_____
_____
_____
_____
_____
_____
_____
_____
_____
_____

Write a letter to yourself about the worst mood you've ever been in. What triggered it, and how did you get over it?

_____

_____

_____

_____

_____

_____

_____

_____

_____

_____

_____

_____

_____

_____

_____

_____

_____

_____

_____

Write a letter to yourself about who you would spy on if you could spy on anyone in the world without them knowing.

_____

_____

_____

_____

_____

_____

_____

_____

_____

_____

_____

_____

_____

_____

_____

_____

Write a letter to yourself about what superpower you'd possess if you could choose one.

_____

_____

_____

_____

_____

_____

_____

_____

_____

_____

_____

_____

_____

_____

_____

Write a letter to yourself about your favorite
thing about springtime.

Write a letter to yourself about one thing you
dislike about summertime (if anything!).

Write a letter to yourself about your guiltiest pleasure.

Write a letter to yourself about a gift you wish you hadn't given to someone.

Write a letter to yourself about an apology you never gave but now feel like you should have. What would you say to that person?

Write a letter to yourself about the best
experience you ever had at a zoo.

Write a letter to yourself about the very first friend you remember making.

_____

_____

_____

_____

_____

_____

_____

_____

_____

_____

_____

_____

_____

_____

_____

_____

Write a letter to yourself about something your
mom would be surprised to know about you.

_____

_____

_____

_____

_____

_____

_____

_____

_____

_____

_____

_____

_____

_____

_____

_____

Write a letter to yourself about something personal
you told your BFF but later wished you hadn't.

_____

_____

_____

_____

_____

_____

_____

_____

_____

_____

_____

_____

_____

_____

_____

_____

_____

_____

_____

_____

**Write a letter to yourself about what
music means to you.**

Write a letter to yourself about your thoughts on politics. Are you interested in politics?

_____

_____

_____

_____

_____

_____

_____

_____

_____

_____

_____

_____

_____

_____

_____

_____

Write a letter to yourself about which subject you'd love to be magically awesome at in school.

_____

_____

_____

_____

_____

_____

_____

_____

_____

_____

_____

_____

_____

_____

Write a letter to yourself about the person who's had the biggest influence on the person you are today.

Write a letter to yourself about something you can't do until you're an adult that you wish you could do today.

Write a letter to yourself about the cutest outfit
you've ever seen your crush wear.

Write a letter to yourself about a makeover you'd like to give yourself (or someone else). What would you change?

_____

_____

_____

_____

_____

_____

_____

_____

_____

_____

_____

_____

_____

_____

_____

_____

_____

_____

_____

_____

Write a letter to yourself about a time you were especially brave. What happened?

Write a letter to yourself about the scariest
thing you ever had to do.

Write a letter to yourself about a tree house, clubhouse, or
another type of hideout you had (or dreamed about) as a kid.

_____

_____

_____

_____

_____

_____

_____

_____

_____

_____

_____

_____

_____

_____

_____

_____

_____

_____

Write a letter to yourself about the funniest
prank you've ever pulled on someone.

Write a letter to yourself about how you feel about growing up.

_____

_____

_____

_____

_____

_____

_____

_____

_____

_____

_____

_____

_____

_____

_____

_____

_____

_____

Write a letter to yourself about what freaks you out most about becoming an adult.

_____

_____

_____

_____

_____

_____

_____

_____

_____

_____

_____

_____

_____

_____

_____

_____

_____

_____

_____

_____

Write a letter to yourself about one of your school rivals and what first caused the beef between you.

_____

_____

_____

_____

_____

_____

_____

_____

_____

_____

_____

_____

_____

_____

_____

_____

_____

_____

Write a letter to yourself about where you'd go if you did a college semester abroad.

_____
_____
_____
_____
_____
_____
_____
_____
_____
_____
_____
_____
_____
_____
_____
_____
_____
_____
_____
_____
_____

Write a letter to yourself about the language
you'd most like to learn, and why.

Write a letter to yourself about something your parents really care about . . . that you totally don't.

Write a letter to yourself about something you REALLY
wish your parents would stop nagging you about.

_____

_____

_____

_____

_____

_____

_____

_____

_____

_____

_____

_____

_____

_____

_____

_____

Write a letter to yourself about what your perfect Sweet 16 birthday bash would be like.

_____

_____

_____

_____

_____

_____

_____

_____

_____

_____

_____

_____

_____

_____

_____

_____

Write a letter to yourself about the kind of charity you would create if you decided to launch one.

Write a letter to yourself about your favorite flower. Why is it your fave?

Write a letter to yourself about the worst surprise you ever got.

_____

_____

_____

_____

_____

_____

_____

_____

_____

_____

_____

_____

_____

_____

_____

Write a letter to yourself about the most
awesome surprise you ever got!

_____

_____

_____

_____

_____

_____

_____

_____

_____

_____

_____

_____

_____

_____

_____

_____

_____

Write a letter to yourself about the meal you'd most like to learn to cook for someone you wanted to impress (including yourself!).

Write a letter to yourself about who you'd
like to swap places with for a day.

Write a letter to yourself about your BFF's weirdest habit.

_____

_____

_____

_____

_____

_____

_____

_____

_____

_____

_____

_____

_____

_____

_____

_____

_____

Write a letter to yourself about the greatest Fourth of July you can remember.

Write a letter to yourself about what other culture you'd most like to immerse yourself in.

_____
_____
_____
_____
_____
_____
_____
_____
_____
_____
_____
_____
_____
_____
_____
_____
_____
_____

Write a letter to yourself describing your thoughts about cats.

_____

_____

_____

_____

_____

_____

_____

_____

_____

_____

_____

_____

_____

_____

Write a letter to yourself about the thing
you worry about most.

**Write a letter to yourself about a friend
that you kind of . . . don't like that much.**

_____

_____

_____

_____

_____

_____

_____

_____

_____

_____

_____

_____

_____

_____

Write a letter to yourself about your worst heartbreak ever (it doesn't have to be romantic!).

Write a letter to yourself about what you'd do first if you woke up one day with the ability to fly.

Write a letter to yourself about a fairy tale or childhood story that means a lot to you.

Write a letter to yourself about the worst teacher you've ever had.

_____

_____

_____

_____

_____

_____

_____

_____

_____

_____

_____

_____

_____

_____

_____

_____

Write a letter to yourself about what you'd want people to say about you at your funeral.

Write a letter to yourself about your least fave artistic pursuit.

Write a letter to yourself about something you love about snow.

_____

_____

_____

_____

_____

_____

_____

_____

_____

_____

_____

_____

_____

_____

_____

_____

_____

Write a letter to yourself about the celeb you'd most like to have as a BFF.

_____

_____

_____

_____

_____

_____

_____

_____

_____

_____

_____

_____

_____

_____

_____

_____

_____

_____

_____

Write a letter to yourself about the funniest gossip you've ever heard about yourself.

Write a letter to yourself about the meanest
gossip you've ever heard about yourself.

Write a letter to yourself about a rumor you spread about someone else that you wish you could take back.

_____

_____

_____

_____

_____

_____

_____

_____

_____

_____

_____

_____

_____

_____

_____

_____

Write a letter to yourself about where you want to be in ten years.

_____

_____

_____

_____

_____

_____

_____

_____

_____

_____

_____

_____

_____

_____

_____

_____

_____

Write a letter to yourself about what you imagine yourself looking like at age thirty.

_____

_____

_____

_____

_____

_____

_____

_____

_____

_____

_____

_____

_____

_____

_____

Write a letter to yourself about the three qualities you think make a great relationship.

_____

_____

_____

_____

_____

_____

_____

_____

_____

_____

_____

_____

_____

_____

_____

_____

Write a letter to yourself about a type of insect you wish you could wipe off the face of the Earth.

_____

_____

_____

_____

_____

_____

_____

_____

_____

_____

_____

_____

_____

_____

_____

_____

_____

**Write a letter to yourself about
your very first pet.**

_____

_____

_____

_____

_____

_____

_____

_____

_____

_____

_____

_____

_____

_____

Write a letter to yourself about the
worst job you can imagine.

Write a letter to yourself about what kind of business you'd like to start.

_____

_____

_____

_____

_____

_____

_____

_____

_____

_____

_____

_____

_____

_____

_____

_____

Write a letter to yourself about bullying.
Have you ever been bullied?

_____

_____

_____

_____

_____

_____

_____

_____

_____

_____

_____

_____

_____

_____

_____

_____

Write a letter to yourself about the place where you feel most serene.

Write a letter to yourself about your
worst experience in PE or gym class.

Write a letter to yourself about what kind of writer you'd be if you decided to become a writer.

_____

_____

_____

_____

_____

_____

_____

_____

_____

_____

_____

_____

_____

_____

Write a letter to yourself about something in history that upsets you.

Write a letter to yourself about your fave TV or movie villain and what you like (or loathe) about them.

_____
_____
_____
_____
_____
_____
_____
_____
_____
_____
_____
_____
_____
_____
_____
_____
_____
_____
_____

Write a letter to yourself about what you kinda look forward to about old age.

_____

_____

_____

_____

_____

_____

_____

_____

_____

_____

_____

_____

_____

_____

_____

_____

Write a letter to yourself about the
TV-show world you'd most like to
live within.

Write a letter to yourself about the strangest gift you've ever gotten.

_____

_____

_____

_____

_____

_____

_____

_____

_____

_____

_____

_____

_____

_____

Write a letter to yourself about your astrological sign. Do you believe in that stuff?

_____

_____

_____

_____

_____

_____

_____

_____

_____

_____

_____

_____

_____

_____

_____

_____

Write a letter to yourself about psychics.
Would you ever want to go to one?

_____

_____

_____

_____

_____

_____

_____

_____

_____

_____

_____

_____

_____

_____

_____

_____

_____

Write a letter to yourself about a time
you experienced déjà vu.

Write a letter to yourself about a time you felt ashamed of yourself.

Write a letter to yourself about a secret language you invented as a kid—or one you'd like to make up now!

Write a letter to yourself about one of your fave childhood games.

Write a letter to yourself about
your favorite singer.

Write a letter to yourself about your best experience at a doctor's office.

Write a letter to yourself about a moment of simple joy that wasn't necessarily based on anything external.

_____

_____

_____

_____

_____

_____

_____

_____

_____

_____

_____

_____

_____

_____

_____

_____

Write a letter to yourself about your ultimate comfort food.

Write a letter to yourself about a time you felt like you couldn't wait for the day to just be over already.

_____
_____
_____
_____
_____
_____
_____
_____
_____
_____
_____
_____
_____
_____
_____
_____
_____
_____

Write a letter to yourself about the technological gadget you can't live without.

_____

_____

_____

_____

_____

_____

_____

_____

_____

_____

_____

_____

_____

_____

_____

_____

Write a letter to yourself about the best
playlist you've ever made. What's on it, and
when do you listen to it?

**Write a letter to yourself about
your favorite Web site.**

Write a letter to yourself about a time you got mad at someone for no reason.

**Write a letter to yourself about soul mates.
Do you believe in them?**

_____

_____

_____

_____

_____

_____

_____

_____

_____

_____

_____

_____

_____

_____

_____

_____

_____

_____

Write a letter to yourself about what you'd do during your ultimate bubble bath. Would you eat, drink, or read anything while you were in there?

Write a letter to yourself about what bugs you
most about the guys in your class.

Write a letter to yourself about what bugs
you most about the girls in your class.

Write a letter to yourself about a time a teacher went out of his or her way to make you feel special.

Write a letter to yourself about a time you totally bombed a test at school. How'd you feel about it?

_____

_____

_____

_____

_____

_____

_____

_____

_____

_____

_____

_____

_____

_____

_____

_____

_____

Write a letter to yourself about what it means to be truly happy.

_____

_____

_____

_____

_____

_____

_____

_____

_____

_____

_____

_____

_____

_____

_____

_____

_____

_____

Write a letter to yourself about what it means to be a true friend.

Write a letter to yourself about what you're
most likely to spend your allowance on.

_____

_____

_____

_____

_____

_____

_____

_____

_____

_____

_____

_____

_____

_____

_____

_____

Write a letter to yourself about the kind of monster
that scares you most (ghost, witch, zombie, dragon?).

Write a letter to yourself describing your thoughts on reality TV.

_____

_____

_____

_____

_____

_____

_____

_____

_____

_____

_____

_____

_____

_____

_____

_____

_____

_____

Write a letter to yourself about your fave board game (and whether you like board games in general).

_____

_____

_____

_____

_____

_____

_____

_____

_____

_____

_____

_____

_____

_____

_____

_____

Write a letter to yourself about how you feel about video games.

_____

_____

_____

_____

_____

_____

_____

_____

_____

_____

_____

_____

_____

_____

_____

_____

Write a letter to yourself about a time you won something. How'd you feel afterward?

Write a letter to yourself about what kind of
teacher you'd be if you ever decided to teach.

Write a letter to yourself about the most annoying
celebrity out there and why they bug you so much.

_____

_____

_____

_____

_____

_____

_____

_____

_____

_____

_____

_____

_____

_____

_____

_____

Write a letter to yourself about what you'd most want your crush to say to you.

_____

_____

_____

_____

_____

_____

_____

_____

_____

_____

_____

_____

_____

_____

_____

_____

_____

_____

Write a letter to yourself about your favorite song . . .
that reminds you of someone else.

Write a letter to yourself about what your
life might be like without the Internet.

Write a letter to yourself about working out.
Do you like it? Hate it? Ignore the entire concept?

Write a letter to yourself about your
least favorite word.

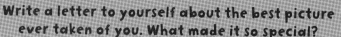

Write a letter to yourself about the best picture ever taken of you. What made it so special?

_____

_____

_____

_____

_____

_____

_____

_____

_____

_____

_____

_____

_____

_____

_____

_____

_____

_____

_____

Write a letter to yourself about the best pic you ever took of someone else. Why was it great?

_____

_____

_____

_____

_____

_____

_____

_____

_____

_____

_____

_____

_____

_____

_____

_____

_____

_____

Write a letter to yourself about an animal behavior you'd most like to magically possess—think purring, barking, flying, roaring, whatever.

_____

_____

_____

_____

_____

_____

_____

_____

_____

_____

_____

_____

_____

_____

_____

_____

_____

_____

Write a letter to yourself about how you feel about thunderstorms.

Write a letter to yourself about your grandparents.

Write a letter to yourself about a time you felt like you had an instant bond with someone, like you'd known them for a really long time, even if you hadn't.

Write a letter to yourself about a friend you hope will stay in your life forever. What kind of adventures can you see yourself having with them when you're old?

_____

_____

_____

_____

_____

_____

_____

_____

_____

_____

_____

_____

_____

_____

_____

_____

_____

Write a letter to yourself about how your parents met. If you don't know, ask!

_____

_____

_____

_____

_____

_____

_____

_____

_____

_____

_____

_____

_____

_____

_____

_____

_____

Write a letter to yourself about a time when you should have stopped to help someone or ask if they were OK, but didn't.

_____
_____
_____
_____
_____
_____
_____
_____
_____
_____
_____
_____
_____
_____
_____
_____

Write a letter to yourself about the best year
of your life so far. Why was it so great?

_____

_____

_____

_____

_____

_____

_____

_____

_____

_____

_____

_____

_____

_____

_____

_____

_____

_____

Write a letter to your five-year-old self. What advice would you give the younger you about growing up?

Now write a letter to your nine-year-old self!

_____

_____

_____

_____

_____

_____

_____

_____

_____

_____

_____

_____

_____

_____

_____

_____

_____

Write a letter to yourself from the perspective of your favorite crush. Get creative!

Write a letter to yourself about how you feel about flying. What's the best or worst airplane flight you've ever been on (if you've been on any)?

_____

_____

_____

_____

_____

_____

_____

_____

_____

_____

_____

_____

_____

_____

_____

_____

_____

_____

_____

Write a letter to yourself about your biggest regret.

Write a letter to yourself about the illness you're most afraid of getting.

_____

_____

_____

_____

_____

_____

_____

_____

_____

_____

_____

_____

_____

_____

_____

_____

_____

Write a letter to yourself about a funky accessory you wish you could pull off.

Write a letter to yourself about a time when you stopped liking a crush. What caused it?

Write a letter to yourself about a time you felt
you were going to explode from excitement.

_____

_____

_____

_____

_____

_____

_____

_____

_____

_____

_____

_____

_____

_____

_____

_____

Write a letter to yourself about a time you felt like you were going to burst with nervousness.

_____

_____

_____

_____

_____

_____

_____

_____

_____

_____

_____

_____

_____

_____

_____

_____

_____

_____

_____

Write a letter to yourself about a time when your feelings changed about a buddy.

Write a letter to yourself about
what would happen during your
most perfect day.

_____

_____

_____

_____

_____

_____

_____

_____

_____

_____

_____

_____

_____

_____

_____

_____

_____

_____

Write a letter to yourself about the weirdest thing a stranger has ever said to you.

Write a letter to yourself about a movie or a
song everyone seems to love . . . except you.
Why aren't you into it?

_____

_____

_____

_____

_____

_____

_____

_____

_____

_____

_____

_____

_____

_____

_____

_____

_____

Write a letter to yourself about your favorite childhood babysitter. Do you remember any especially fun or awesome experiences you had with them?

_____

_____

_____

_____

_____

_____

_____

_____

_____

_____

_____

_____

_____

_____

_____

_____

_____

_____

_____

Write a letter to yourself about your favorite kind of soda.

Write a letter to yourself about what you like and dislike about getting sick and staying home from school.

_____

_____

_____

_____

_____

_____

_____

_____

_____

_____

_____

_____

_____

_____

_____

_____

_____

Write a letter to yourself about a time you fell down in a humiliating fashion.

_____

_____

_____

_____

_____

_____

_____

_____

_____

_____

_____

_____

_____

_____

_____

_____

_____

Write a letter to yourself about a time someone
made fun of you for something you wore.

Write a letter to yourself about the best
cat video you've ever seen. EVER.

Write a letter to your forty-year-old
self all about who you are today.

_____

_____

_____

_____

_____

_____

_____

_____

_____

_____

_____

_____

_____

_____

_____

_____

Write a letter to yourself detailing all the reasons why you deserve to get everything on your wish list for the holidays.

_____

_____

_____

_____

_____

_____

_____

_____

_____

_____

_____

_____

_____

_____

_____

_____

_____

Write a letter to yourself about the meaning of life.

Write a letter to yourself about your thoughts on marriage. Is getting married something you want to do one day? Why?

Write a letter to yourself about how it feels in your body when you really love someone.

_____

_____

_____

_____

_____

_____

_____

_____

_____

_____

_____

_____

_____

_____

Write a letter to yourself about how it feels
in your body when you really detest someone.

_____

_____

_____

_____

_____

_____

_____

_____

_____

_____

_____

_____

_____

_____

_____

_____

_____

Write a letter to yourself about your fave artistic pursuit.

_____

_____

_____

_____

_____

_____

_____

_____

_____

_____

_____

_____

_____

_____

_____

_____

_____

_____

_____

Write a letter to yourself about your favorite jeans.

Write a letter to yourself about your favorite thing to eat for breakfast.

Write a letter to yourself about something your best friend does that grosses you out.

_____

_____

_____

_____

_____

_____

_____

_____

_____

_____

_____

_____

_____

_____

_____

_____

_____

_____

Write a letter to yourself about the nastiest
thing you've ever tasted.

Write a letter to yourself about external appearances. Do looks matter to you?

Write a letter to yourself about a time you remember happily looking up at the stars.

_____

_____

_____

_____

_____

_____

_____

_____

_____

_____

_____

_____

_____

_____

_____

_____

_____

_____

Write a letter to yourself about the ocean.

Write a letter to yourself about your worst
experience at the hairdresser.

_____
_____
_____
_____
_____
_____
_____
_____
_____
_____
_____
_____
_____
_____

Write a letter to yourself about camping.
Ever been? Do you like it?

_____

_____

_____

_____

_____

_____

_____

_____

_____

_____

_____

_____

_____

_____

_____

_____

_____

_____

Write a letter to yourself about your favorite thing to order at Starbucks.

Write a letter to yourself about the hair color
you kinda wish you had. If you love your
current color, awesome! Write about that.

Write a letter to yourself about a time an idol or mentor disappointed you.

_____

_____

_____

_____

_____

_____

_____

_____

_____

_____

_____

_____

_____

_____

_____

_____

_____

_____

Write a letter to yourself about the movie world you'd most like to live inside.

Write a letter to yourself about the first book you remember making you cry.

_____

_____

_____

_____

_____

_____

_____

_____

_____

_____

_____

_____

_____

_____

_____

_____

_____

Write a letter to yourself about a cartoon character that sort of reminds you of yourself.

Write a letter to yourself about a time a crush did something that bummed you out.

_____

_____

_____

_____

_____

_____

_____

_____

_____

_____

_____

_____

_____

_____

_____

_____

_____

_____

_____

_____

Write a letter to yourself about a time you ate so much you felt sick.

_____

_____

_____

_____

_____

_____

_____

_____

_____

_____

_____

_____

_____

_____

Write a letter to yourself about a time
someone yelled at you for no reason.

Write a letter to yourself about the most
beautiful sight you can ever remember seeing.

Write a letter to yourself about something you secretly
want your parents to know ... but can't tell them.

_____
_____
_____
_____
_____
_____
_____
_____
_____
_____
_____
_____
_____
_____
_____
_____

Write a letter to yourself about the
smell of coffee. Does it gross you out or
smell good to you?

Write a letter to yourself about a time you excelled at something you'd thought you wouldn't be that good at.

Write a letter to yourself about a time you bombed
something you thought you'd be good at.

_____

_____

_____

_____

_____

_____

_____

_____

_____

_____

_____

_____

_____

_____

_____

_____

_____

Write a letter to yourself about the kind of homework you like and hate the most.

_____

_____

_____

_____

_____

_____

_____

_____

_____

_____

_____

_____

_____

_____

_____

_____

_____

Write a letter to yourself about how you feel about art class.

_____

_____

_____

_____

_____

_____

_____

_____

_____

_____

_____

_____

_____

_____

_____

_____

_____

_____

Write a letter to yourself about the genre of music you'd most want to listen to every day for the rest of your life.

_____

_____

_____

_____

_____

_____

_____

_____

_____

_____

_____

_____

_____

_____

_____

Write a letter to yourself about a time you waited too long to do something and then missed your chance.

_____

_____

_____

_____

_____

_____

_____

_____

_____

_____

_____

_____

_____

_____

_____

_____

_____

_____

_____

_____

Write a letter to yourself about the most important thing you learned in school—something that changed how you saw the world.

Write a letter to yourself about the most important thing you learned from someone who isn't a teacher.

Write a letter to yourself about the best
party you've ever been to.

**Write a letter to yourself about what you're
most grateful for in life.**

Write a letter to yourself about the worst name you've ever been called and how it made you feel.

_____

_____

_____

_____

_____

_____

_____

_____

_____

_____

_____

_____

_____

_____

_____

_____

_____

_____

Write a letter to yourself about a
random act of kindness you witnessed
and how it made you feel.

_____

_____

_____

_____

_____

_____

_____

_____

_____

_____

_____

_____

_____

_____

_____

_____

_____

_____

_____

_____

_____

Write a letter to yourself about the craziest thing you've ever (willingly) done.

_____

_____

_____

_____

_____

_____

_____

_____

_____

_____

_____

_____

_____

_____

_____

_____

_____

_____

_____

_____

Write a letter to yourself about your parents' jobs—
would you ever want to follow in either of
their footsteps, work-wise?

_____

_____

_____

_____

_____

_____

_____

_____

_____

_____

_____

_____

_____

_____

_____

_____

_____

_____

Write a letter to yourself about what instrument you'd play if you could play anything.

Write a letter to yourself about how it feels on the first day back to school after summer vacation.

_____

_____

_____

_____

_____

_____

_____

_____

_____

_____

_____

_____

_____

_____

_____

_____

_____

Write a letter to yourself about the family you imagine having one day.

_____

_____

_____

_____

_____

_____

_____

_____

_____

_____

_____

_____

_____

_____

_____

_____

Write a letter to yourself about three of your biggest life goals and how you can make them happen.

_____

_____

_____

_____

_____

_____

_____

_____

_____

_____

_____

_____

_____

_____

_____

_____

_____

Write a letter to yourself about a time someone caught you in a lie. How'd you feel?

_____

_____

_____

_____

_____

_____

_____

_____

_____

_____

_____

_____

_____

_____

_____

_____

Write a letter to yourself about your favorite dessert.

Write a letter to yourself about a time one of your parents
(or another family member) made you totally crack up.

_____

_____

_____

_____

_____

_____

_____

_____

_____

_____

_____

_____

_____

_____

_____

Write a letter to yourself about your favorite aspect of winter (if there is one!).

Write a letter to yourself about how you feel after a good cry.

_____

_____

_____

_____

_____

_____

_____

_____

_____

_____

_____

_____

_____

_____

Write a letter to yourself about what
you imagine your first romantic
relationship being like.

_____

_____

_____

_____

_____

_____

_____

_____

_____

_____

_____

_____

_____

_____

_____

_____

_____

_____

_____

Write a letter to yourself about someone you know who truly loves you, even if they don't always say it.

_____

_____

_____

_____

_____

_____

_____

_____

_____

_____

_____

_____

_____

_____

_____

_____

_____

_____

Write a letter to yourself about the store you'd most like to work in if you got a job at the mall one summer.

_____

_____

_____

_____

_____

_____

_____

_____

_____

_____

_____

_____

_____

_____

Write a letter to yourself about amusement parks. Do you like 'em?

_____

_____

_____

_____

_____

_____

_____

_____

_____

_____

_____

_____

_____

_____

_____

_____

_____

_____

Write a letter to yourself about how long the school year would be if you had it your way.

_____

_____

_____

_____

_____

_____

_____

_____

_____

_____

_____

_____

_____

_____

_____

_____

_____

Write a letter to yourself about a musical artist who reminds you of who you are now . . . or who you want to be later!

_____

_____

_____

_____

_____

_____

_____

_____

_____

_____

_____

_____

_____

_____

_____

_____

_____

Write a letter to yourself about the idea that money can't buy happiness. Do you agree?

Write a letter to yourself about something you learned in school that doesn't feel AT ALL applicable to your life.

Write a letter to yourself about something you like to do with your hands.

_____

_____

_____

_____

_____

_____

_____

_____

_____

_____

_____

_____

_____

_____

Write a letter to yourself about the creepiest creature that lives in the deep sea.

_____

_____

_____

_____

_____

_____

_____

_____

_____

_____

_____

_____

_____

_____

_____

_____

_____

Write a letter to yourself about a mythic creature you actually kind of believe in (or want to believe in).

_____

_____

_____

_____

_____

_____

_____

_____

_____

_____

_____

_____

_____

_____

_____

_____

_____

_____

Write a letter to yourself about a skill you wish was taught in school (but isn't!).

Write a letter to yourself about what
makes a good mom or dad.

_____

_____

_____

_____

_____

_____

_____

_____

_____

_____

_____

_____

_____

_____

_____

_____

_____

Write a letter to yourself about how you feel
about your siblings—or lack of them.

Write a letter to yourself about space aliens. Do you believe in them? What do you think they look like?

_____

_____

_____

_____

_____

_____

_____

_____

_____

_____

_____

_____

_____

_____

_____

Write a letter to yourself about a time
you broke a promise to someone.

Write a letter to yourself about a time someone
broke a promise to you.

Write a letter to yourself about your favorite childhood cartoon.

_____

_____

_____

_____

_____

_____

_____

_____

_____

_____

_____

_____

_____

_____

_____

_____

Write a letter to yourself about a time a dream came true.

_____

_____

_____

_____

_____

_____

_____

_____

_____

_____

_____

_____

_____

_____

_____

_____

_____

Write a letter to yourself about what it's like when you can't sleep at night. What do you do?

Write a letter to yourself about your favorite nature sound (crickets chirping, the wind blowing, the ocean crashing, you get the picture!).

Write a letter to yourself about the best joke you've ever invented (or the best joke you've ever heard).